This book belongs to

_____

_____

Welcome to my illustrated world of steampunk fantasy houses!

Relax and explore a world of wonderfully complex and beautifully detailed pen-and-ink illustrations–all waiting to be brought to life through color.
For artists and budding architects of all ages.

The artworks in my books are based on illustrations I have drawn over my years as an artist. The designs are filled with imaginative detail whilst remaining fun and accessible to younger colorists.

See more at rjhampson.com

 russelljamesart

Published by Hop Skip Jump
PO Box 1324 Buderim Queensland Australia 4556

First published 2023.
Copyright © 2023 R.J. Hampson.

All Rights Reserved. Without limiting the rights under copyright reserved above, no part of this publication may be reproduced, stored in or introduced into a retrieval system, or transmitted, in any form or by any means (electronic, mechanical, photocopying, recording or otherwise), without the prior written permission of both the copyright owner and the above publisher of this book. The only exception is by a reviewer who may share short excerpts in a review.

ISBN: 978-1-922472-29-8

Using this book

Find a quiet place away from distractions. Relax and immerse yourself in the process of coloring as you explore the details of each fantastic illustration.

This book is best suited to color pencils or markers. Wet mediums should be used sparingly. Slide a card behind the illustration you are coloring to avoid marker bleed through.

Find fresh coloring pages by signing up to the R.J. Hampson newsletter. Get free downloadable pages and updates on new books at -

rjhampson.com/coloring

THE BIRDHOUSE

THE BIRDHOUSE

THE POWERHOUSE

THE LIGHTHOUSE

THE MOBILE HOME

MRS HOBSON WALKS THE DOG

THE PIRATE HOUSE

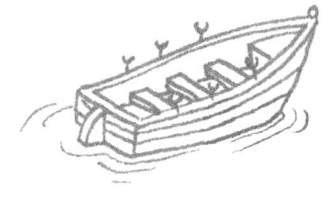

THE LIGHTHOUSE NO. 2

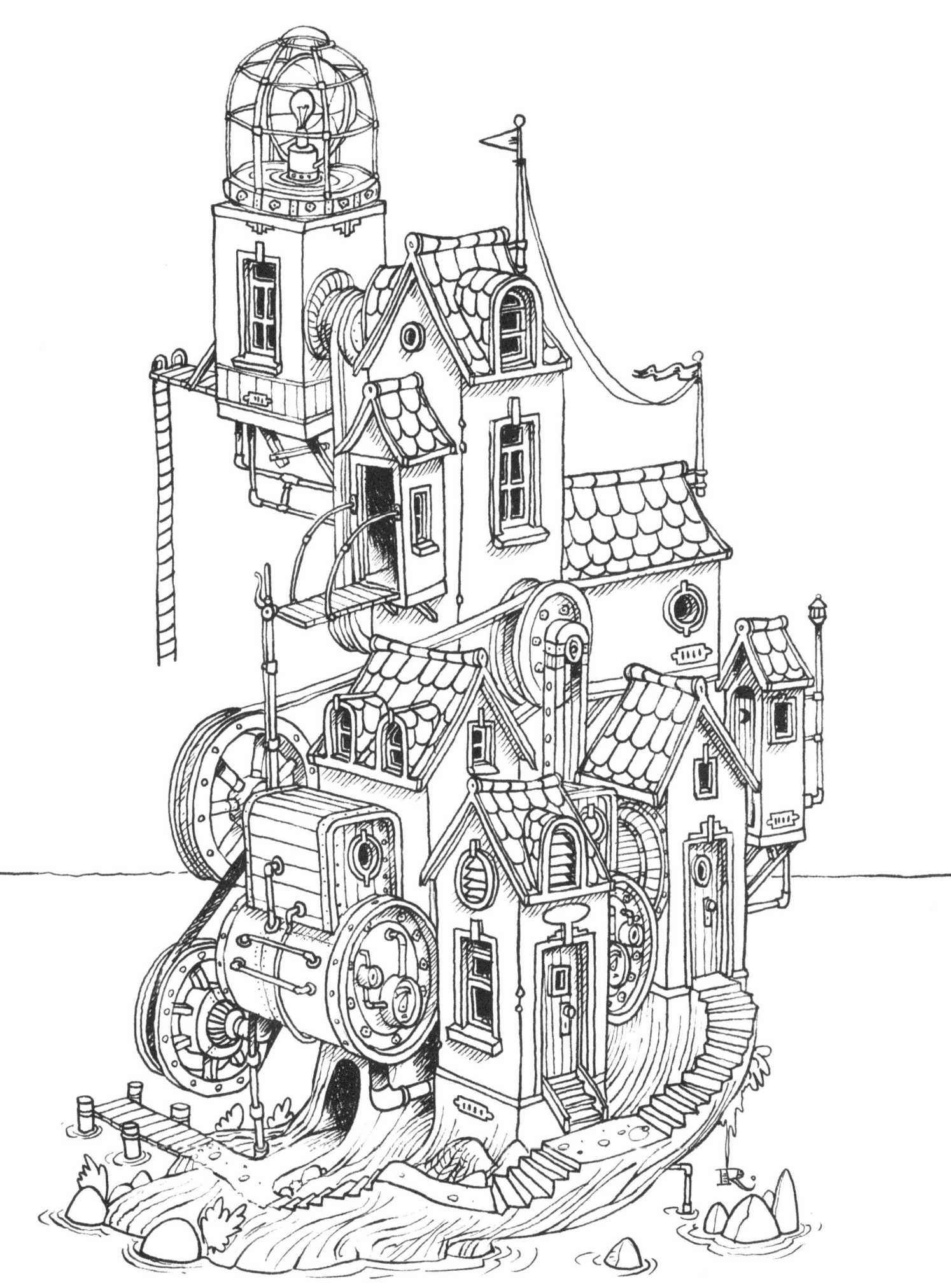

THE BEARS & THE BEES

THE CLOUD TEMPLE

E-7 GOVERNMENT INSTALLATION

JACK'S HOUSE

JACK'S HOUSE

THE SAFE HOUSE

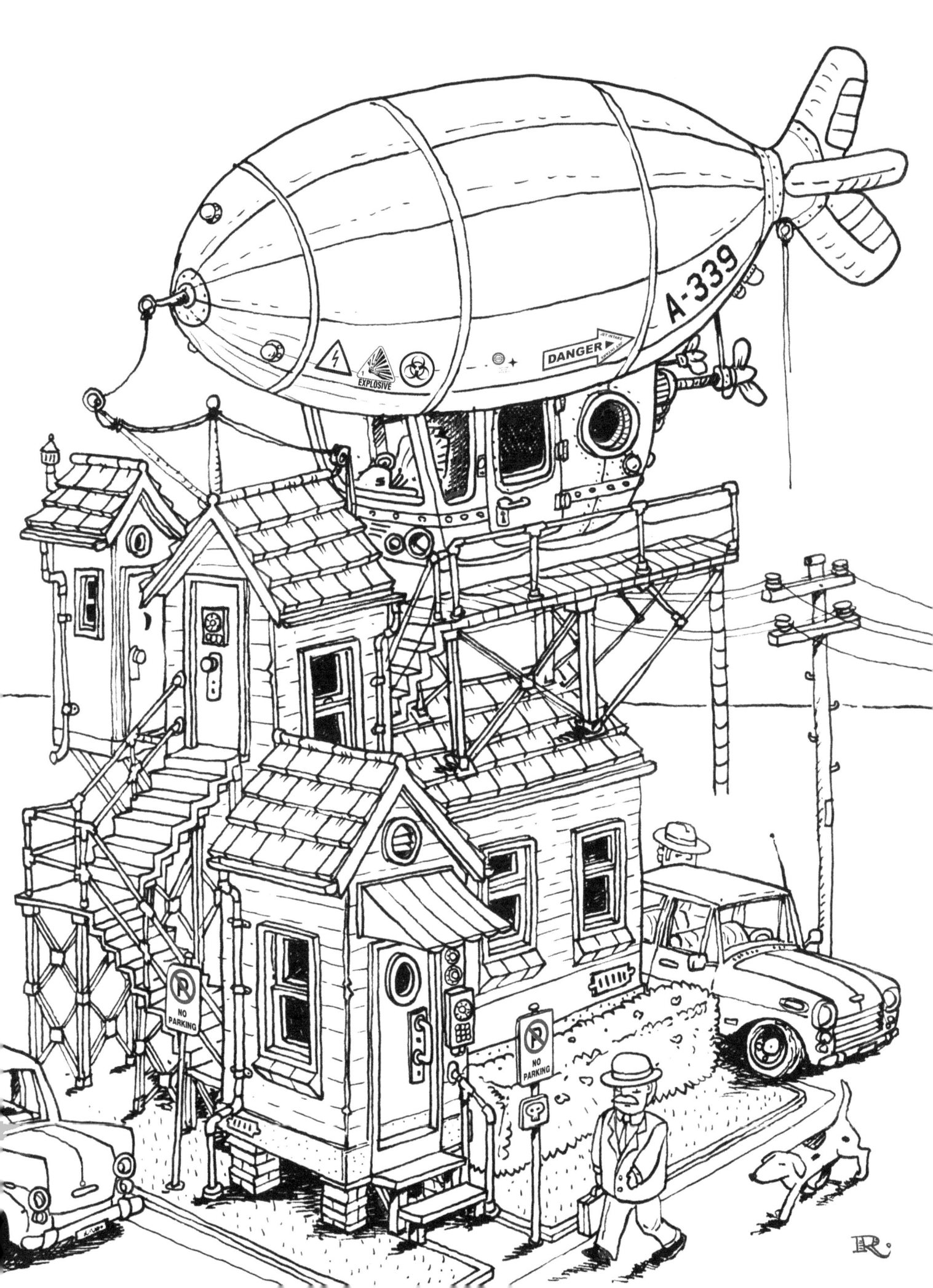

THE SUBURBAN FRACKING HOUSE

THE POWERHOUSE NO. 2

THE TOXIC HOUSE

THE TREE HOUSE

THE WATER HOUSE

WATER HOUSE NO. 2

THE VICTORIAN STEAM HOUSE

THE JUNGLE HOUSE

JUNGLE HOUSE NO. 2

THE DRAGON HATCHERY

THE POOL HOUSE

THE BARBER'S HOUSE

JUNGLE HOUSE NO. 3

Unlock bonus material!

Find new coloring pages by signing up to Russell's newsletter.
Get free downloadable pages and updates on new books at -
rjhampson.com/coloring

Thanks for choosing this coloring book.
If you enjoyed it, please consider leaving a review.
It will help to let more people in on the experience
plus you'd certainly make this illustrator very happy!

Published books in this series

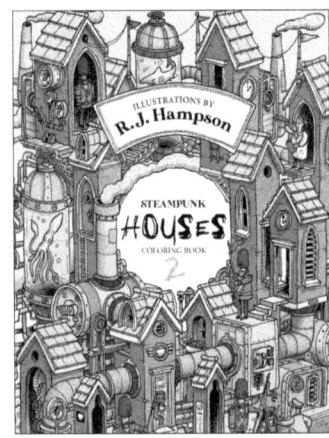

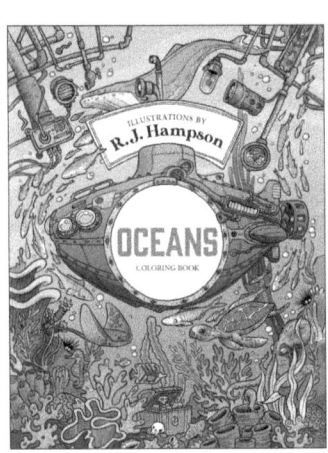

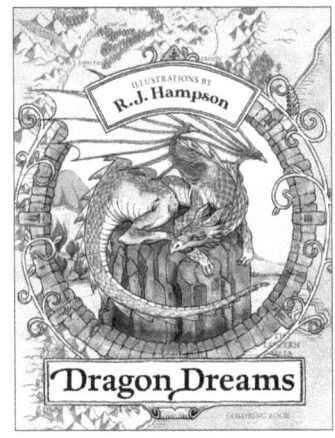

See flip-throughs and new releases at **rjhampson.com**

www.ingramcontent.com/pod-product-compliance
Lightning Source LLC
Chambersburg PA
CBHW041221240426
43661CB00012B/1110